born in lockdown

born in lockdown

a selection of poems

quentin smith

q2upublishing

Copyright © 2021 by Quentin Smith, who asserts the moral right to be identified as the author of these poems. All rights reserved.
No part of this publication may be reproduced, without prior written permission of the publisher.

First Printing, 2021

ISBN 978-1-5272-8754-9

This book is dedicated to Jacqueline
making my sun rise since 1982

Any profits derived from book sales will be donated to
Alzheimer's Society.

Dementia touches so many lives these days.
If you have enjoyed this book, I am truly glad, but please also
consider buying a copy for a friend.
Thank you so much, Q.

running out

i'm running out of patience
i'm completely out of luck
i've put them on my shopping list
but deliveries are stuck

the drivers can't get moving
the tunnel's all backed up
they've confiscated sandwiches
authority's cracked up

my wit is also at its end
and i'm running short of time
been on the phone to Asda
but i'm caller number 9

i'm fresh out of ideas
they've been in short supply
they've half-baked ones at Lidl
but "conditions will apply"

i'm a little light on detail
i'm low on self-esteem
i don't know what it retails for
but it lives on aisle 15

but someone's had the last laugh
and now i'm quite confused
they said they'd keep some back for me
so i'm really not amused

i've ordered optimism
i'm told it's rather good
you dab a bit behind each ear
if you feel misunderstood

but i can't get hold of any
it's coming in next week
so i might just have to settle
for a bottle of upbeat

i've Googled bulldog spirit
but Amazon's sold out
they've got an old stiff upper lip
but it's not enough to pout

i'm feeling out of sorts
i'm running out of road
i could use a little extra spark
but there's none at this postcode

the kids are climbing up the wall
home schooling doesn't work
my six year old's been driving
our nine year old berserk

i've checked the government guidance
saying holidays are banned
but the man from Travis Perkins says
they can deliver sand

so we're digging up the garden
and putting in a beach
i'll sit in my bikini
and try my best to teach

and in July we'll rent it out
on that Airbnb
we've ordered some exotic plants
and a 10 year old palm tree

so i reckon we'll be cleaning up
once this summer's through
when the voice at Asda's telling me
i'm caller number two!

christmas on ice

this anxious society
this social anxiety
keeping our distance
at safety's insistence

standing in queues
emotions askew
clinging to life
infections run rife

all sitting tight
garnering resentment
can't sleep at night
bereft of contentment

non-essential retail
stays open all hours
intensive care fills
the national mood sours

then it's all aboard
the packed Covid train
standing room only
for the variant strain

the tunnel is closed
police on the borders
you'll need to disclose
and follow the orders

we all need to shout
and let off some steam
as Christmas in tiers
was not in our dreams

our plans are in tatters
but keep them on ice
because what really matters
is we don't pay the price

and when vaccines clear trials
be glad that you're here
to lift a cold vial
to those you hold dear

words

crammed in together they slouch in a bunch
lazing like dogs who've had too much lunch
timid like children who wake in the night
hiding their faces away from the light

bumping together with one eye still closed
steadily becoming a bit more composed
ready for shaping into a design
awaiting assembly in legible lines

new thoughts are scribbled then quickly erased
but slowly an order begins to take place
handfuls of sentences start to emerge
a river of words is beginning to surge

sending messages to say we're alive
words paint the pictures we want to describe
scratching a note when danger's around
revealing a secret but making no sound

announcing the arrivals of babies and trains
they trickle down pages like droplets of rain
settling neatly they sit side by side
printed on broadsheets and hung out to dry

puzzling commuters with cryptical clues
blowing down streets wearing yesterday's news
written in books in fonts of all sizes
double entendres in cunning disguises

illegible letters in spidery scrawls
political slogans graffitied on walls
lit up at night on motorway signs
slim ones that squeeze behind enemy lines

words that we crave to hear of us said
words that we hear that fill us with dread
words carved on stones when loved ones depart
words memorised and held in our hearts

words can get twisted and people confused
words can disarm and be misconstrued
words can be tender and soothing and wise
words can be poignant and help us realise

words bring the context to life's lessons learned
words we'll remember when pages have turned
words tell us stories with beginnings begun
words provide closure to endings undone

headed to connemara

i'm headed to Connemara where i surely won't be found
i'll lie low and rest my head upon her holy ground
i'll find an empty and make a home until it's safe to stand
i'll pen some words and sew some grain and work her loving land

for i have sinned and made a crime so heinous and so bold
i've run away to Ireland my possessions i have sold
i'll walk the hills and speak to none that flitter 'cross my path
i'll keep a dog for company and warm her by the hearth

and if you see me please don't tell a soul or sell me out
i'm on the run from madness of that there's little doubt
there's understanding knowledge and cleverness i'm sure
but where it hides at times like these is desperately obscure

so if you don't mind i'll linger here a longer while yet
i'll hunker down and burn my peat and keep out of the wet
please write to me to let me know when sanity's returned
but until then i'll stay right here and watch the fire burn

let's reach out

i dreamt i died, and all the words i should have said
gathered in my head.
they made no sound, not wishing to expound,
they just brooded and held their ground.

but the message was plain, no reason to explain,
they wanted more, tired of being ignored,
frustrated in their silent world,
they longed to be unfurled.

we all have flaws,
and there are cracks in everything,
but that's how the light gets in.

right now we're looking in, divided and apart,
but with words flowing we might start to look out,
to end the vacuum, reconnect and stop the drought.

so let's reach out,
let's all touch base,
let's phone a friend,
let's track and trace
and get in touch,
eschew regret,
and meet beyond the next sunset.

minds eye mountain

i take a long walk to comfort my mind
it helps me to process and passes the time
decluttering my head from all the surreal
the clearer the view the better i feel

checking the forecast avoiding the rain
the questions, the judgements, the lies and the pain
i just need to figure which way is up
life will seem better when i get to the top

leaving behind all the chattering cafes
thoughts turning on once i get on my way
up at the peak there's no soul around
only the wind and the birds make a sound

i stand up tall, stretch my hands to the sky
feeling each vertebra let out a sigh
i turn my head so the wind hits my face
suspending the stress from this moment's grace

up here i close my eyes and can see
fast flowing rivers and acres of trees
vast golden plains of ripe swaying wheat
blue oceans framing the land where they meet

breezes push weeds over dry desert floors
saguaros host sparrows from winters before
a million diamonds that stud the night sky
shoot at each other but nobody dies

with an emptier head i see far and wide
gain some perspective and feel less confined
there's room now to think and conjure some words
with freedom to roam away from the herd

it's not just the ruckus that others might make
the clatter and buzz that keeps us awake
sometimes our own inner thoughts can invade
needing the stillness to calm the tirade

on my way down i try to steer clear from
irrelevant hubbub i don't need to hear
already planning the next big ascent
to the minds eye mountain i love to frequent

street '71

i sit by the window
watching our street
the comings and goings
a bird's-eye view seat

no sign of the milkman
and it's quarter to eight
our silver tops missed
no creak of the gate

my brother's had Nesquik
and used the last drop
Dad's told him before
but he can't seem to stop

when he gets to the kitchen
there'll be hell to pay
if there's nothing to pour
on Dad's Special K

the road sweeper's been
and gathered the leaves
he swept a big pile
but they're gone in the breeze

he toiled like a Trojan
huffing and puffing
now they're back whence they came
and it's all been for nothing

here comes the postman
a glint in his eye
letters for seven
and a parcel for five

i hear a bell ringing
the rag and bone man
he's traded his horse
for a blue Transit Van

that trusty brown mare
all battled and scarred
has finally gone off
to the glue maker's yard

he gathers the castoffs
from next door but one
a rusty old cooker
that must weigh a ton

The Sun is delivered
the front page is ripped
page three is exposed
all photoed and stripped

the paperboy Martin
he should take more care
tearing the cover
and leaving her bare

the man two doors down
is walking his hound
he's looking elsewhere
as it shits on the ground

he checks for onlookers
before leaving the scene
passing a sign that reads
"keep our streets clean"

my transistor's dialled
into radio one
Marc Bolan's singing
about riding a swan

i'm not sure the meaning
but i'm loving the song
yet 6 years from now
that man will be gone

a foot on the stairs
Mum's checking on me
i leap into bed
before she can see

she writes out a note
to say i've got flu
but just so you know
between me and you

i'm swinging the lead
not as ill as i seem
cos tomorrow there's football
and i'm picked for the team

take your difference

he came out of nowhere and headed towards town
"keep walking mister and don't turn around,
we don't suffer fools or strangers round here"
but he carried straight on with a flea in his ear

he strolled with a grace and seemed light as air
his features were sharp and framed by long hair
he seemed quite untroubled by the hurt and abuse
but what he was thinking was hard to deduce

everyone stared as he rounded main square
his skin a shade darker, his coat was threadbare
he stood a bit taller, his eyes a soft grey
and as he drew closer the folks backed away

he climbed up the steps and the crowd pushed and shoved
he held up his hands to the dark sky above
the people were restless, they shouted and coughed
then he started to speak, his voice deep and soft

"it's written in scripture that i came here before,
and many have prayed that i'd visit once more
my message seemed simple but you're clearly confused
so i'm back as requested and there's no time to lose

the wars that you started you've said in my name
the bombing and killing and passing the blame?
it's just not important who's right and who's wrong
your children will deal with the mess when you're gone

so send me an email, a text or a tweet
when you've space for me on your "things to do" sheet
but in the meantime, please share what you've got
with those who have less and those who have naught

show people kindness as if they're your own
provide warmth and shelter for those with no home
give help to the poor, they can't spend your tears
and call me again in two thousand years"

the people looked angry as he stepped from the stage
they hustled and jostled and showed him their rage
their message grew louder from the faintest of starts
"take your difference and be gone from these parts"

getting better

i thought i'd send you a box of bees
assuming you were on your knees
to provide you with a certain buzz
as a gift of bees normally does
but from what i've seen you're doing fine
and keeping a positive state of mind
which is great!   however..

i couldn't afford you more than five
which is a long way short of half a hive
but it stays within the rule of six
so it doesn't contravene the politics
but demand for pets has gone sky high
and now bees cost more than dragonflies

so…   not wishing to sound absurd
my second thought was a box of birds
to keep you company while you're in town
and amuse you when you're feeling down
and when you're worried in the night
they'd keep you strong and help you fight

but the sign above the nurses station
says birds are against the regulations
as they find the distancing too hard
and security has had them barred
and anyway you'd never sleep
with all their constant chirpy cheep

so all i have is this poor poem
encouraging you to keep on going
i'm just a friend that you've inspired
telling you you're so admired
and hoping that it keeps you strong
to surf the waves that come along

time on our hands

while we have this time
let's try to solve this climate crime
this planet's in trouble
and we can't keep pretending we live in a bubble.

i've been trying to find
answers to questions that circle my mind
i'm willing to learn
about what we should grow and what we can burn.

we have to take stock
the fact that we're here really isn't a shock
it's time to get real
by making more progress and a lot less ordeal.

so let's cut through the tape
our world's seen enough of its resources raped
what's on our list?
how do diesel and coal power emissions persist?

and while we're here
can we make plastic in oceans disappear?
that would be ace
but leaving it there would be a disgrace.

so who's willing to lift?
this planet requires a paradigm shift
we need to act now
and summon all the strength our bodies allow
because if we don't
these negligent governments sure as hell won't.

swanage bay

i sleep on the hill and see the dawn break
and savour the peace until they're awake
from Peveril Point and across Swanage Bay
torn clouds come ascudding and white horses play

later we might take a stroll down the pier
we'll have a fish supper and a pint of best beer
an ice cream to finish, we're easy to please
then we'll all fall asleep to the sound of the breeze

i dreamt of a family just like my own
when i was at war and a long way from home
i sit up here now and my dreams have come true
and i pinch myself that i have all of you

tomorrow we'll all take a walk up the path
if Wiggles gets muddy we'll give her a bath
we'll race to the lighthouse and gaze out to sea
then back to the 'van for a nice cup of tea

but tomorrow can wait as i'm not in a rush
the blackbirds are chirping and breaking the hush
i think i'll just lie here a little while more
and wait for the stirring of those i adore

everything fell out

unnecessary acronyms
corporate legalese
constipated dialect
filling with unease
spectacular vernacular
terms of some redoubt
uncaptured enraptured
words come tumbling out

avoiding sentencing
                listing
        to
    the
left
boxed in cooped up
linguistically bereft
starch fronted upjumpted
occasionally obtuse
restraining containing
verbally abstruse

scripture stricture
unravelling below
bypassing conformity
letting it all go
unbound ungagged
shouting it all out
unfettered language
writing without doubt

debunking unjunking
spreading it below
unblocking defrocking
freeing up the flow
myth-busting untrusting
turning on the light
illuminating corners
and providing some insight

explicit complicit
getting up the spout
slithering and slathering
and warbling about
scrambling rambling
need to disengage
thawing melting
and dripping off the pa
                g
                e

days by the coast

shall we go to the coast tomorrow
assuming the weather is fine?
just jump in the car and tootle straight off
around a quarter past nine?
we'll park in the lane, get a free space
and find a bench on the prom
pick up a paper on the way through
and beat the incoming throng.

i'll make us some sandwiches wrap them in foil,
there's Mother's Pride in the bin
hard boil some eggs, a big flask of tea
and the Eccles Cakes from the tin.
remember the man with the deckchair last year
the one you needed to teach?
i'll put our basket on the back seat
with a rug to spread on the beach.

your coat's on the peg, your stick's by the door
but you're still nowhere to be seen
but then i glance at the empty chair
and remember the hospital scene.
sometimes i'm really annoyed that you've gone
leaving me here all alone
i'm lonely and although they're not far away
our children have lives of their own.

i miss not having your hand to squeeze,
letting me know it's ok
i miss not telling you things that i've seen
when we sit at the end of the day.
we'd reminisce about times gone by
fond memories of our yesteryear
the dances with friends, "it was much better then"
and the change you got from a beer.

football on Saturday, you in your chair
checking the scores for the pools
a few years ago six draws in row
yet somehow we managed to lose?
on Sundays you'd set a big fire in the hearth
while i fixed the scones and the tea
we'd sit side by side and watch Songs of Praise
with a blanket over our knees.

there's so much to tell you, things that i've seen
so much you've already missed
another birthday card's been forgotten
another grandchild not kissed.
so many things i wished that i'd said
they all line up in my head
and when it gets dark and i put down my book
there's only one light by the bed.

i wouldn't have swapped you for anyone dear
no one came close to compare
it didn't matter to me what i did
as long as i knew you were there.
there are days when i think i still hear you
opening the door for the post
but the days that i cherish most of all
were those days that we spent by the coast.

we used to do things

we used to do things
like go places make noise and leave traces
we didn't have to think
just check-in and chill then head for a drink

we're shadows of ourselves
blank faces stare out from now vacant shells
we're ghosts from our pasts
b-movie actors who've been badly miscast

cue clouds scudding past
cue "there's no protection from wearing a mask"
"it's clear up ahead"
and "shuffle off Granny we'll be needing your bed"

now we're all NHS fans
hammering away on our old pots and pans
but who's banging the drum
next time their wages and budgets get done

all we get is "it's just common sense"
as the spoils are trousered by the hapless front bench
where it seems there's no shortage of milk and honey
but there wasn't enough for the children's lunch money

so just give us some truth
were too old for lies and too long in the tooth
and stop all the spin
the lies and the bullshit are all wearing thin

we know it's corrupt
when government contract awards are abrupt
they're massive amounts
and those responsible should be held to account

so lets get it sorted
we need an enquiry and get this reported
and don't leave it late
or you're going to need your eyes testing mate

do you fancy going to the pictures tonight ?

watching old movies at home has been fun
but for me the cinema beats it hands down
the experience has always had me beguiled
right from the outset when i went as a child

on Saturday mornings for a shilling a head
we'd go to the movies while Mum stayed in bed
we'd load up on pick & mix ready to scoff
kids cheering loudly as the lights were turned off

a few years later you'd pick up the phone
hoping she'd answer and her Dad wasn't home
if she said yes you'd get spruced up nice
a shower, a comb and a splash of Old Spice

invariably the chat would go something like
"do you fancy going to the pictures tonight
they're showing Rocky, my friend says it's great"
then you pray that you don't bump into your mates

over the years the scene's been the same
watching the stars make their fortune and fame
in iconic movies with girlfriends or wives
now those films trace the track of our lives

we'd create false birthdays for certificate 14's
we saw Blazing Saddles at the Screen on the Green
queuing up for Star Wars and not getting in
then scanning the ocean for a big white shark fin

then Taxi Driver and Midnight Express
De Niro and Foster right up with the best
the Deerhunter scene playing Russian roulette
with Christopher Walken's as good as it gets

how about the ones where you jumped in your seat
the Exorcist, Carrie, Nightmare on Elm Street
something for everyone funny or sad
fantastical, hopeful, pathetic or bad

they created characters to suit every mood
E.T and Woody, the Joker, the Dude
Gromit or Tommy or Marge from Fargo
Maximus, Gollum and Inspector Clouseau

Bill the Butcher and Indiana Jones
or Kevin McCallister stuck Home Alone
there's Holly Golighty and Marty McFly
Princess Leia and Pesci's wise guys

some go by numbers like the Magnificent 7
or 9 to 5 and Ocean's 11
there's 9 1/2 weeks and 12 Angry Men
or Catch 22 and Bo Derek's 10

after we'd quote the lines the stars say
like Harry Callaghan's "punk make my day"
and Travis Bickle "are you talking to me"
or John Travolta and his "royale with cheese"

so many great partnerships over the years
when Harry met Sally brought laughter and tears
Newman and Redford as Butch and Sundance
or Jack and Rose's Titanic romance

listing your favourites is such a hard job
i loved the Godfather and the Goodfellas mob
or Bonnie and Clyde with Beatty and Faye
or the Usual Suspects and Keyser Soze

and some films just simply cannot be missed
like Close Encounters and Schindler's List
Forrest Gump and the Shawshank Redemption
Psycho, Rain Man and Lost in Translation

i'm hoping la la land can normalise soon
and we free ourselves from our lockdown cocoons
we'll turn off our phones and try not to cough
and go see a movie that blows the doors off

i want to

i want to freeze this moment
i want to stop the clock
i want to never lose you
i want to turn the lock
i want to lay here with you
i want to stay the night
i want to live beside you
i want to make it right
i want to keep the world out
i want to hide away
i want to make it special
i want to mark this day
i want to always see you
i want to not lose sight
i want to help protect you
i want to hold you tight
i want to watch you sleeping
i want to walk the beach
i want to trace your footsteps
i want to stay in reach

i want to grow old with you
i want to not regret
i want to paint the sunset
i want to not forget
i want to live a lifetime
i want to rest in peace
i want to die beside you
if this world should cease

lost at tesco's

as i tied my laces a voice in my ear
said "excuse me, have we lost something dear ?"
an elderly lady was looking concerned
so i drew myself up and softly returned
"yes" I said "we've lost many dear things
and i worry about what tomorrow might bring
responsible governance is absent you see
the plot has been lost and so has the key

right now we're losing our race against time
as hospitals fill and we stand in our lines
we've begun to lose patience, our shit, and our way
but sadly no weight since last Christmas Day"
looking puzzled and a little aghast she said
"have you been waiting for someone to ask?
you poor old soul my heart does go out but
i'm sure they'll turn up once you're out and about"

but i'd only just started so I carried straight on
"and trust" i said "that seems to have gone
we've lost the dressing room, the remote, and the ark
our mojo, our socks, our love and our spark
we're losing our hair, and our heart's desire
knowing when to step in and when to retire
the ability to surprise and our naked ambition
our minds, our community and all inhibitions

we won the battle but we've lost the war
another good man and the girl next door
we lost our innocence a ways back when
and things have been tricky for losers since then
we've lost vital seconds on life's alarm clock
sweating incidentals as time goes tick tock
we lost our identity quite some time back
i guess social media's to blame for all that

our planet is losing it's fight against change
so everyone loses but no one's to blame
we've all lost a yard and i've lost my drive
along with the ability to still be surprised
so i'll finish my rant now if you'll forgive
before i start losing the will to live"
she studied her wrist, "gosh it's past noon
Edith will worry if i'm not with her soon"
but under her breath i heard plain as day
"that poor man's lost it" as she hurried away.

i'll see you on the 1st

Once we've got this sorted and can head out unafraid,
we'll try to find our clubs or buy some new from
Taylor Made. We won't expect to score that well
just enjoy the getting out, remembering to tip a cap
to those that are without.

But before old habits start to show let's appreciate the view,
the ozone air, the fresh cut grass, the white against the blue.
The sound of seagulls cawing as the breeze
moves through the dunes, and the shadows as they lengthen
on those perfect afternoons.

We'll strike some sweetly, some less so and try hard
not to swear, we'll hit some perfect drives and then
some wedges of despair. The 6 iron to the 5th that hits
the stick and bounces off, is only part and parcel of this
love hate game of golf.

And afterwards we'll go inside and buy ourselves a beer,
three of us will try and give the fourth something to cheer.
Like fishermen we'll talk about the putts that should
have dropped, and how we'd all shoot 75
if only the rain had stopped.

Sound advice is handed out so each one may improve
"a steeper angle of attack should get you in the groove".
And "if you turned your shoulders more and flattened
out the plane", but we'll all come back the next day
and swing the same again.

So settle back, do your drills, and in time sure enough,
we'll be searching on the 14th for a Titleist in the rough.
And afterwards we'll gather in the bar and slake our thirst,
so keep yourself in good shape and i'll see you on the 1st.

warmth of the underground

woke up again on the subway floor
vaguest memory of the night before
slipping in and out of sleep
ain't got a dream that's worth the keep

passer by puts a coffee down
asks if this is my home town
i'd tell him i've been here a week
but my throat's too dry and my voice won't speak

blows rained down till i'd take no more
deserted my post to end his war
i'll find someplace i can't be found
lying 'gainst the warmth of the underground

people paid to hear me sing
i felt the joy my voice would bring
a million downloads and shining lights
those smiling faces on concert nights

but time moved on and life turned down
my smile erased redrawn a frown
now tears streak down and age my face
no longer feel part of this human race

i'll haul myself up from this cold hard street
been knocked down but there's no defeat
the dawn is rising on a brand new day
the sun's gonna chase my clouds away

i'll find the courage still got some left
shake myself up and catch my breath
gonna fight for those paralysed by fear
and give them the strength to persevere

london's calling

a nightingale calls in St. James' Park
the sun's not up to puncture the dark
it's 5am, there's a chill in the air
as bin men collect around Cavendish Square

bakers' vans, bread straight from the oven
delivered to shops and the people who govern
market porters are hefting their crates
at Nine Elms, Smithfield and New Billingsgate

where buyers for restaurants ignoring advice
huddle round tea as they haggle the price
down on the river the big wheel turns
bikers and joggers have calories to burn

taxi drivers with livings to make
search for a fare as the City awakes
beneath our feet rumble passenger trains
burrowing deep with the sewers and drains

bodies decant along pavements like blood
clogging the arteries and pooling like mud
high up above us buildings touch skies
the tip of The Shard steals the sunrise

inhaling breathing sustaining and green
the parks are the lungs that keep the air clean

as kids we'd hop on a red bus and roam
up the Monument or round St. Paul's dome
we'd climb Tower Bridge and cross Waterloo
then jump the back fence and bunk in the Zoo

later we'd go to the pubs and get loud
drinks underage with the East Finchley crowd
shopping at Camden and going on dates
The Clash at the Roundhouse then back to a mate's

that was back then before London evolved
the city now buzzes and everything's sold
a million restaurants open all hours
in hotels and basements and ivory towers

a pint in Soho's a fun place to start
it's pubs are edgy and beat like a heart
the Dog and Duck or the Old Nellie Dean
or head to Ronnie's for the latest jazz scene

listen to the banter up at the bar
from lovers and poseurs and wannabe stars
the Cockneys and Mockneys touting their wares
and the bit of fluff that lives up the stairs

it's musical prowess is second to none
think Bowie, The Stones and of course Elton John
compelling artists to write down their pearls
like Waterloo Sunset or West End Girls

spawning princes and poets both famous and rich
some born in Mayfair and some in Shoreditch
Nightingale, Dickens, Byron and Keats
history stalks these old cobbled streets

go stand on the heath and take in the view
from Greenwich Park to the gardens at Kew
on a clear day you'll see the South Downs
while the Thames glistens and splits the foreground

so as soon as it's safe let's go for a cruise
or row down to Putney and get on the booze
'cos you can keep your Sydney's your Rio's and Rome's
it's London for me, the place i call home.

ideas

thoughts occurring in the night
ideas that hatch and switch a light
the best laid plans to undertake
are dreams forgotten when i wake,
lost in the hubbub of the day
they wriggle loose and drift away.
throughout my mind i dredge and trawl
desperately seeking some recall
elusive yet within my reach
like lessons i am yet to teach.

during meetings i'd nod and smile
to interject was not my style
my smart ideas were worth a crack
but i impeded and held them back,
when what i really should have done
was given them a chance to run,
releasing them into the wild
reintroduced and reconciled
to roll their sleeves and have a scrap
with all their other-worldly crap.

all those things i should have said
kept their counsel and stared ahead
like actors who never spoke
or comedians without a joke,
tight lipped they just enjoyed the ride
reluctant to step outside
umbrellas that stayed wrapped tight
i'd take them home with me at night
glad to have escaped the showers
they'd languish in the darkened hours.

but following good friends' advice
enabled me to recognise
that my ideas were just as good
as others in the neighbourhood,
and it really had been quite a waste
not to let them have their taste
of freedom, and be off my chest
pitching them with all the rest,
allowing myself to be exposed
not caring whether they're opposed.

hank and the phoenix

the bell rang out both loud and clear upon the red front door,
and the door creaked slowly open like a thousand times before,
a creature entered the premises and walked across the floor,
she wore a brightly coloured tail that one could not ignore.

and when the creature spoke her voice was elegant yet frail,
"could you kindly check if they have sent me through my mail?"
the man behind the counter looked world weary and quite pale,
"please would you have a seat, i'll need some more detail."

"what's your name?" he asked of her as he peered over his specs,
she looked a little pensive, "the spelling's quite complex,
it means to rise again, it starts with p and ends in x,
and isn't really spelt the way one usually expects."

the Postmaster looked confused and not a little blank,
and then he asked a question "Miss, please may i be frank?,
i'd hate for you to think me rude or even worse a crank,
so let me introduce myself to you, my name is Hank."

for many years it felt like Hank had drifted in a trance,
but he knew that this might be his one and only chance,
and he did not wish to lead the Phoenix on a merry dance,
so he quickly grasped the nettle without a second glance.

"if you are indeed a Phoenix as you have just said,
then within your grasp lie special powers or so i think i've read.
i know this really can't be true and i may have been misled,
but the legend states you have been known to even raise the dead?"

the creature turned her head away and seemed a bit put out,
"it's true this reputation does follow me about,
but i like to keep my profile low of that there's little doubt,
for in twenty years this is the only day that i've been out."

the Phoenix stared into Hank's chest and her eyes filled up with tears
"i can see deep within your heart that you've missed your wife for years.
i am willing to banish you of all your pains and fears.
and for taking good care of my mail there will be no arrears."

Hank jumped straight out of his seat not knowing what to say,
"could you really do that Miss, what would I have to pay?"
"don't answer that!" he quickly said, "i'd give this shop away!
if i could spend with her another hour of one day."

"don't worry you may keep your shop no payment would i need,
your heart has demonstrated that you are worthy of this deed,
only your true love and kindness are needed to succeed,
now i'll summon up my powers and your wife she will be freed."

so the Phoenix asked the man to close his eyes and not to peek,
and from her eyes ten silver tears gathered on her cheek,

and as each tear dropped down upon Hank's head from her beak,
a strange sound came from deep within and the Phoenix began to speak.

she gurgled like a babbling brook running full with morning dew,
and all at once a mist rose up and turned the room bright blue,
the windows began to shake and the dust and papers flew,
and then the mist subsided and Hank's wife came into view.

her hair was of the deepest brown and her dress a brilliant white,
and the smile that danced across Hank's face showed his sheer delight,
"i thought that you were lost forever but now i've seen the light"
and the Phoenix bowed down gracefully and flew off into the night.

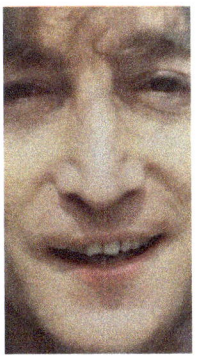

get busy living

life is what happens while you're busy making plans
a wise man's words sent to help us understand
to choose what's important, sort the wheat from the chaff
to live in the moment, to smile and have a laugh

forty years gone can you imagine what he'd say
if he walked right in through those doors today
as we lurch between lockdowns and isolation
d'you think he'd shed a tear for his old birth nation?

he'd impress upon our leaders to give us some truth
and grade them with a U with much room to improve
the mind games they've played throughout this whole year
need to stop so these vaccines can assuage our fear

so let's beat around no longer putting things off
not talking straight and sweating small stuff
let's start over again and put things right
and hopefully that gets us all through the night

we could sit and watch the wheels and just let it all be
but a working class hero is someone to heed
so even though he's gone his statement still demands
that we get busy living, while we're busy making plans

southwold

we park up and pour out and wrap ourselves well
and wander the dunes as the sea boils and swells
a wind from the east chases sand up the beach
while dogs pursue rabbits down holes they can't reach

our cold stinging cheeks are quick to turn red
as tears blur our view of the ramshackle sheds
on past the kiosk serving hot rolls and tea
watching kite surfers take off round the quay

turning for home the town looms into view
the seafront and lighthouse are etched against blue
we're back soon enough in the ebb and the flow
already planning the next time we'll go

don

mix onions, worcester and ketchup in a pan
cook it down until it's like jam,
a teaspoon of sugar and vinegar to taste
stir it around until it's like paste

this is what he taught us to do
marinade the sausages 'til the flavour gets through
a squirrel whisperer with a glint in his eye
a sailor, a gardener, a helluva guy

a husband a father a grandad with a crew
quick with a nickname or a joke or two
which beer can i get you i asked of him once
"pick me out a nice one" was his jolly response

up to his knees in mud thick and smelly
he plucked me and Ted from our stuck fast wellies
around the large pond a crowd followed our cause
before setting us down to a hero's applause

when time was up he'd drive me back home
"always change down before the bend in the road"
in that beige Cortina of which he was proud
with his driving gloves on and the music played loud

he came to this world without much to show
and left us all wishing he didn't have to go
he'll be up there now sailing on the blue
but keeping one eye on our bbq

autumn resolutions

Right around this time of year when leaves depart the bough,
they make their way towards the ground and i make a solemn
vow. Never shall i moan again that the days became
too warm, that the grass grew up too quickly and i had
to mow the lawn.

While damp spores assail my nose and feet squelch in the
ground, colours turn from vibrant green to every shade of
brown. Beneath my feet gathers up the shed from every tree,
as nature weaves its patchwork quilt of crunchy twig debris.

And as robins peck at worms that slither through the moss,
and squirrels forage winter stores, i mourn the daylight lost.
And just before the first frost bites down upon the land,
i'll take myself an inventory and find out where i stand.

I made a promise to myself to be a better friend,
to take some time to get to know our neighbours at the end.
I vowed to do more exercise and eat a little less,
and give some of my excess to people in distress.

So before the last golden leaf can flutter to the floor,
and beavers fix their dams and make them stronger than
before, i'll sow some winter barley from the seed i stored last
year and thresh it when it's malty and mash it into beer.

And before this year is over i'll say myself a prayer, despite
the fact i don't believe there's anybody there. I'll ask him
for a cure for Covid before Christmas is through, and pledge
him all the tea in China and two barrels of me brew.

five years gone

he brought us five years, now five years have gone
the rebel the starman, how brightly he shone
the thin duke, aladdin and old major tom
inventing his guises and turning us on

he was unique, his sound and his vision
influencing iggy and joy division
numan and gaga, pixies and reed
all took a leaf from his avant-garde lead

he sold the world and threw darts in our eyes
and wrote us the songs where we break down and cry
he turned on our lights in our million hordes
from ibiza to warsaw and the cold norfolk broads

but since he's been gone we've lost ground control
there's no ice cream parlours down this rabbit hole
there's pressure on people, and people on streets
and it feels like we're strangers each time we meet

so pull up the seat with the clearest of views
and tune in the station to the six o'clock news
some people will say, "but how could they know"?
but we're all unpaid extras in the freakiest show

so if you feel life's taking you nowhere
and your golden years have dissolved in the air
they've stopped opening doors and pulling your strings
then think our hero and the dolphins that swim

sometimes there's nothing to keep us together
wild is the wind that brings in this weather
but he was the nazz now he's up in the stars
drinking cold milkshakes with the spiders from mars

sligo

pitter patter comes the rain
splishing splashing down the drain
the endless leaves they flutter down
landing lightly on the ground
steadily the rain it pours
turning dark the grey stone walls
overflowing the mossy gutters
and running off the window shutters
but inside a fire is painting faces
shapes appear then leave no traces

the north wind calls beneath my door
come walk with me upon the moor
wild and free ben bulben stands
towering high above the sands
miles downwind a horse is ridden
the sound it carries, the rider hidden
the waves froth higher up the beach
lapping the rocks within their reach
chasing gulls to a higher ledge
meeting the rain at the water's edge

two boots stand ready by the door
patiently waiting to explore
muddy pathways and the damp outside
unaccustomed to being denied
but the kettle sings its urgent song
the pot is warm and the tea is strong
this precious brew won't drink itself
and who could wish for greater wealth.

gone's a long time

shadows run down the old school yard
our hearts get broken our knees get scarred
your number's up when you least expect
so take your chance, have no regrets

some things in life they just won't wait
some times in life you can't be late
when summer's done and your page has turned
your trials are over and your lessons learned

where's the time go we often say
as twilight sweeps the days away
you were always there to make us laugh
your face looks out from photographs

gone's a long time not to have you here
no more chats or beers to share
you never stopped lighting up the room
singing songs and whistling tunes

i thought that you'd be there forever
keeping us calm in stormy weather
now i'm stood underneath this darkening sky
not knowing how to say goodbye

last call for jumbo

we've said our goodbyes to the old jumbo jet
the wheels have touched down on its final descent
the 747's been put out to grass
they've ripped up and cancelled its last boarding pass
those wide bodied planes all laid out in lines
that carried us off to sunnier climbs
will be taxied away and broken for scrap
and now sit in fields like they're having a nap
a long way from perfect and costly to run
they thundered down runways weighing 300 tonnes
i often wondered how they ever took off
the marvels of physics and all of that stuff

since Covid arrived our world's become small
but once we get jabs let's take a long haul
so where shall we fly Nairobi or Rome?
and stop off at Vegas on the way home?
we'll head to the airport 3 hours too soon
swerving round couples on delayed honeymoons
turn left for first class but more likely right
or straight up the stairs to the bar if you like?

the seat belts are clicked and tray tables cleared
the steward says the exits are here, here and here
those stag boys are certain to keep us amused
breaking the seal on their duty-free booze

all round the cabin we're settled in seats
a lady's been round giving out boiled sweets
we tear down the runway, it's all systems go
watching the ground disappear from below
there's old Nervous Nerys in 24B
biting her fingers and spilling her tea
in the seat beside her a Nun thumbs her beads
while flicking the page of the bible she reads
the old man behind has started to snore
despite all the noise it's hard to ignore
the mum with the baby that's cutting its teeth
is dipping its soother in gin for relief

but the Captain is saying we've finished our climb
the trolley's arrived and they''e pouring the wine
so sit back, relax and soon we'll be there
assuming that kid stops kicking your chair
and won't it be great to be back in the clouds
packing our cases and strolling through crowds
we'll soon walk on beaches and cut ourselves loose
if we keep being smart and stick to the rules.

racing sand

the wind throws vowels beneath the door,
come, let me race you to the shore.

we clamber dunes, fine grains filling plastic shoes,
wiry grass flicking knees, as gulls peel sideways on the breeze.

drawn to its edge, the current sucks our heels,
digging them deeper as if on wheels, we fight for balance,

arms stretched like spitfire wings, the sea froths and sings,
as it ferries kelp and broken shell, surfing on the tidal swell.

the low sun shimmers across the peaks, dazzling eyes,
and clearing heads of endless clutter and foolish lies.

the whipped sand outpaces our childish strides,
coarse grains fly, dashing ankles and stinging thighs

it crouches like a hound further on down the beach,
teasing, waiting 'til we come within reach,

then it's off again to repeat the same,
"come chase me to the headland" game.

the tide draws the ocean into rocky channels, filling pools,
creating salty worlds with different rules,

that live until the day is done, when the moon
dismantles the breeze and dissolves the ochre sun.

then home to brush sand from toes, as red rose cheeks
glow over cakes, and tomorrow's plans of friends to meet.

careers office '79

"what sort of job do you want to do?"
i'm 16 years old and about to leave school
like most kids back then i had no idea
we'd do anything just to be free from there

so you fall for the first thing that comes along
muddling and hoping you don't get it wrong
you show up on time and you give it your best
just trying to keep one step ahead of the rest

soon you're clocking on without a thought
you've forgotten all about being an astronaut
those childhood ideas of your grown up self
are put out to grass or placed on a shelf

it's easy to lose the essence of who you are
while Peter Pan's locked in an air tight jar
your life gets busy and the time runs fast
you can feel overwhelmed and yourself miscast

but eventually you might reach a fork in the road
the baggage we accrue becomes a hefty load
but is it ok just to check it all in
reassess retrain and start over again?

you might find fresh skills that are fun to learn
or discover a calling that makes your heart yearn
or rewrite your story in your own new hand
there's time left over for us all to rebrand.

river

long time ago i was shown where to look,
"they're smarter than you with your baited hook".
don't underestimate their desire to be free,
while hiding in the shallows neath the willow tree.

i felt that energy for the very first time,
like my rod plugged itself into a main power line.
bending in an arc and tiring out the trout,
the reel clicking over as the line flew out.

the sun bounced light off the chalk stream bed,
silver streaking by with each turn of its head.
the back of my neck turns red in the sun,
waiting till dusk when the feeding is done.

the river ran clear and fast back then,
teaming with tadpoles and water boatmen.
swifts came swooping as the mayfly hatched,
dreaming one day of that specimen catch.

but today my float was barely disturbed,
nor was the kingfisher's call to be heard.
the river's been arrested by plastic debris,
a shopping trolley floats by the sycamore tree.

the ripples of the damage run far and wide,
and the harm being done is impossible to hide.
the balance of nature has been upset,
but the tide can be turned, there's still time yet.

i dream of teaching my grandkids to fish,
i hope that's an option and not just a wish.
we really must do better next time around,
before the river's dried up and we've run aground.

I started writing poems to relieve the stress and frustration of the last year. The creativity seemed to help. I see it now, but I wasn't aware of that at the time. Words often came to me in the night and sometimes it felt like they weren't mine, they were just there for me to gather and reassemble in the morning. Out of darkness comes light..sometimes anyway.

I didn't set out to create a book, but as the months have gone by and with the encouragement of family and friends they have found a home together here.

I'd like to thank a few people:
My amazing lockdown crew..so supportive, fun and caring x.
RDG, gone a long time. Don, where my cooking began.
Florrie & Reg ..strolling down the pier.
A hat tip to LC for "the crack" on page 18, grhs.
JB x 3 for encouragement, insight, tears and edits.
TC and EH..surfing the waves. MAH, GG , GC and AJB for brotherly love here and across waters. And for all the supportive Facebook and Instagram comments and likes spurring on the process.
Muchas gracias compadres, I hope you enjoy them.

www.ingramcontent.com/pod-product-compliance
Lightning Source LLC
Chambersburg PA
CBHW061234070526
44584CB00030B/4116